America is Great
Patriotic Coloring Book For Kids

Proud of the USA! Color 50 large Pages of United States Symbols and Icons - Independence Day (4th of July) - for Ages 4-8

Rachel Mintz

Updated Edition 2020

Copyright © 2018 Palm Tree Publishing - All rights reserved. No part of this publication may be reproduced, distributed, or transmitted in any form or by any means, including photocopying, recording, or other electronic or mechanical methods, without the prior written permission of the publisher, except in the case of brief quotations embodied in critical reviews and certain other noncommercial uses permitted by copyright law. Images used under license from Shutterstock.com

Look for Rachel Mintz Coloring Books

What is your favorite niche? What would you like to color?

Mandalas | Wildlife | Marine Life| **Portraits** | Dogs | Cats | **Flowers** | Skulls | Gothic | Architecture | Romantic | Texts & Sayings | Ethnic | Steampunk | **Fashion** | Horses | Unicorns | Witches | Horror | Grayscale | Sports | Christmas | Holidays | Kids | Cars | **Motorbikes** | Trucks | Urban | Fairies | **Jewish Holidays**: Passover, Hanukkah, Purim | Safari | Pets |Multicultural | Educational for Kids | Back to School | **Preschool & Toddlers** | Army & Military | Knights & Castles | Dragons | Princesses | Butterflies | Birds | Reptiles | Bible | **Stained Glass** | Abstract | Machines | **Robots** | Space & Science | **Zombies** | Monsters | And many more topics..

Search Amazon for Rachel Mintz coloring + your niche

Scan Code See Military **Digital Coloring Books** (PDF) For Kids & Adults: Tanks, Air Force, Marines, Special Forces and More.. **Instant download!** Color favorite pages again and again..

Abraham Lincoln

Sweet Land of Liberty

Home of the Brave

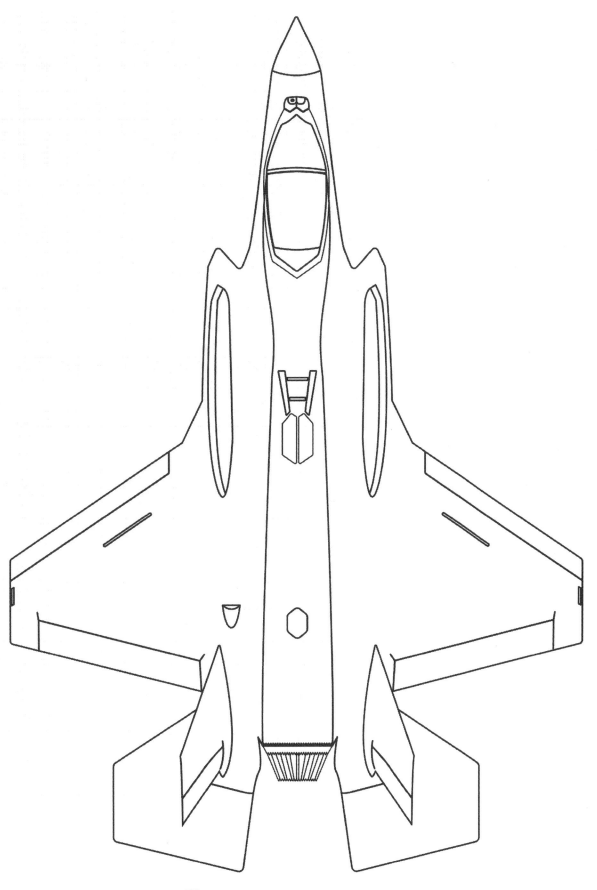

Freedom Is Not Free

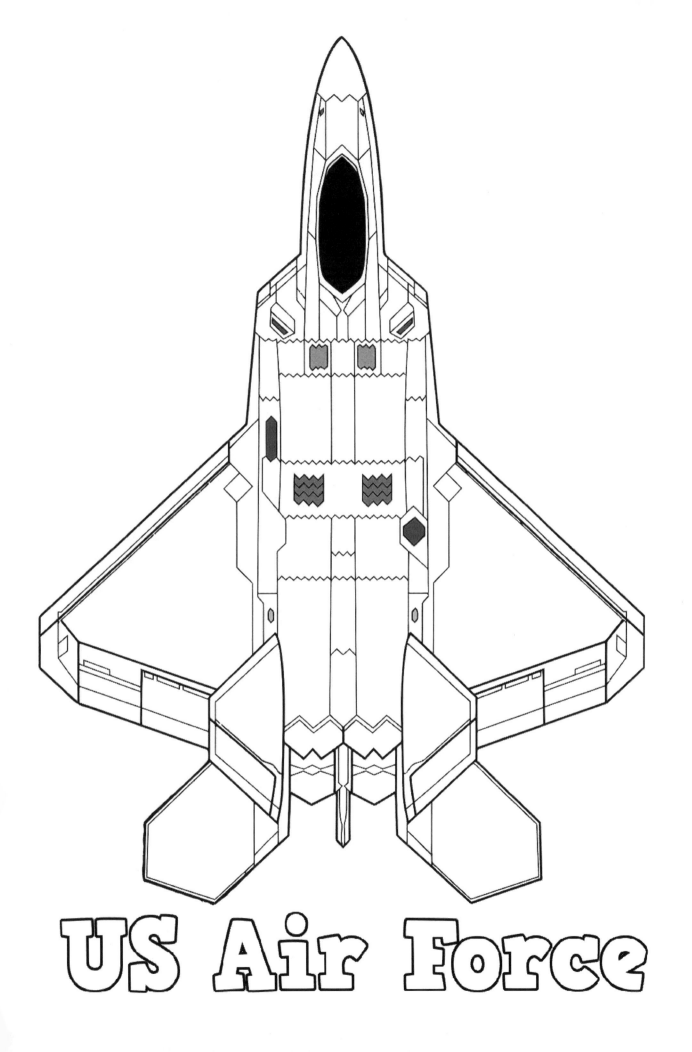

Happy Independence Day

United We Stand

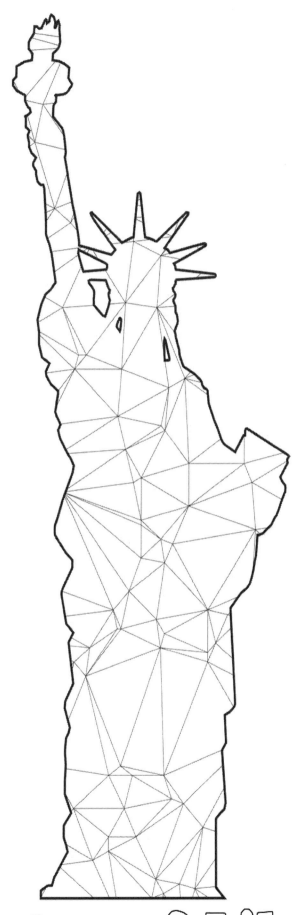

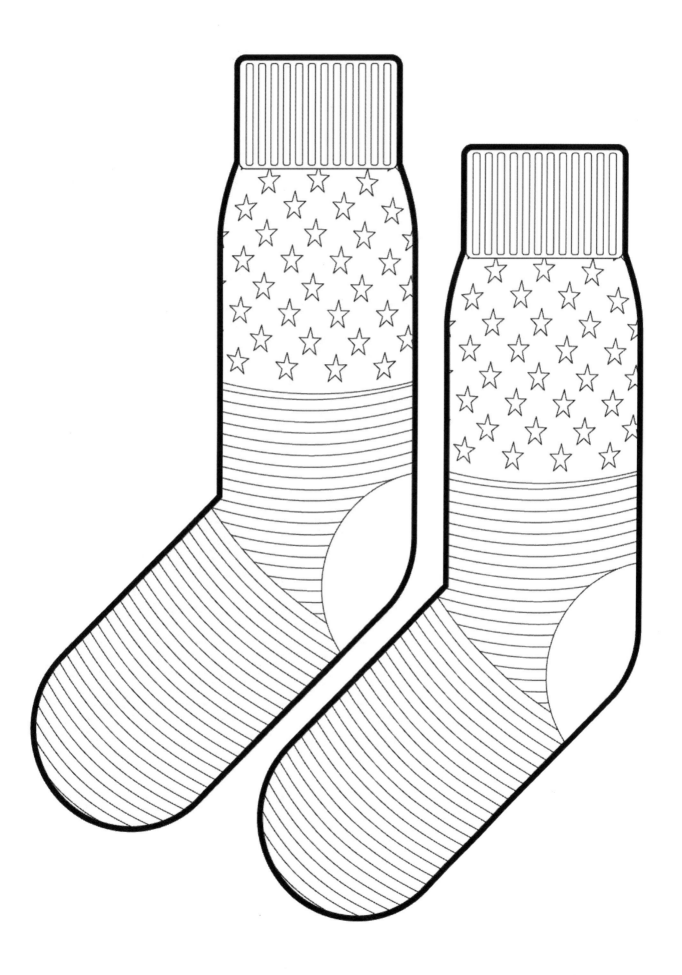

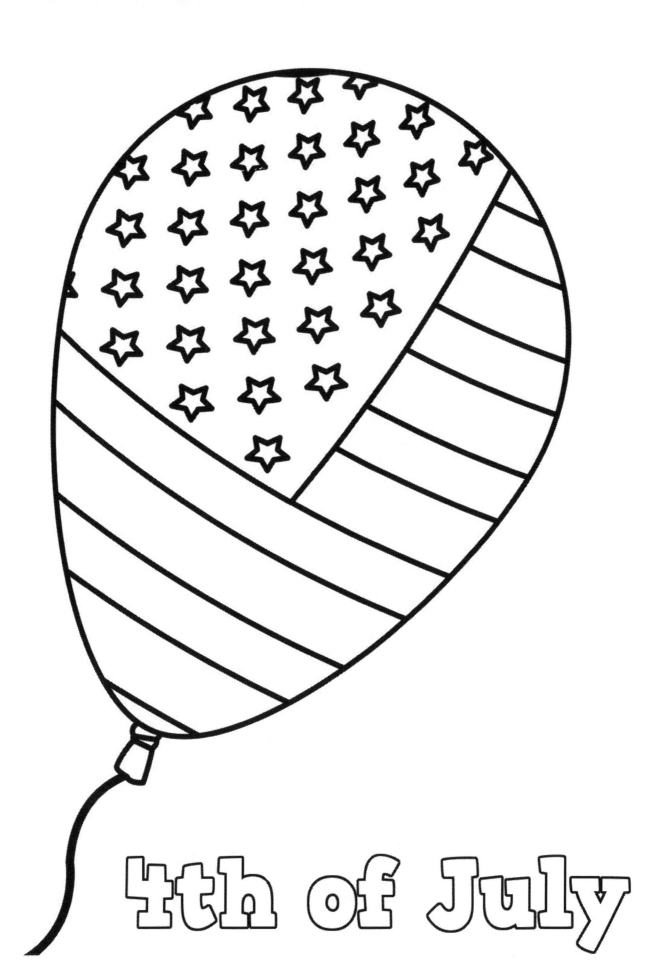

Declaration of Independence

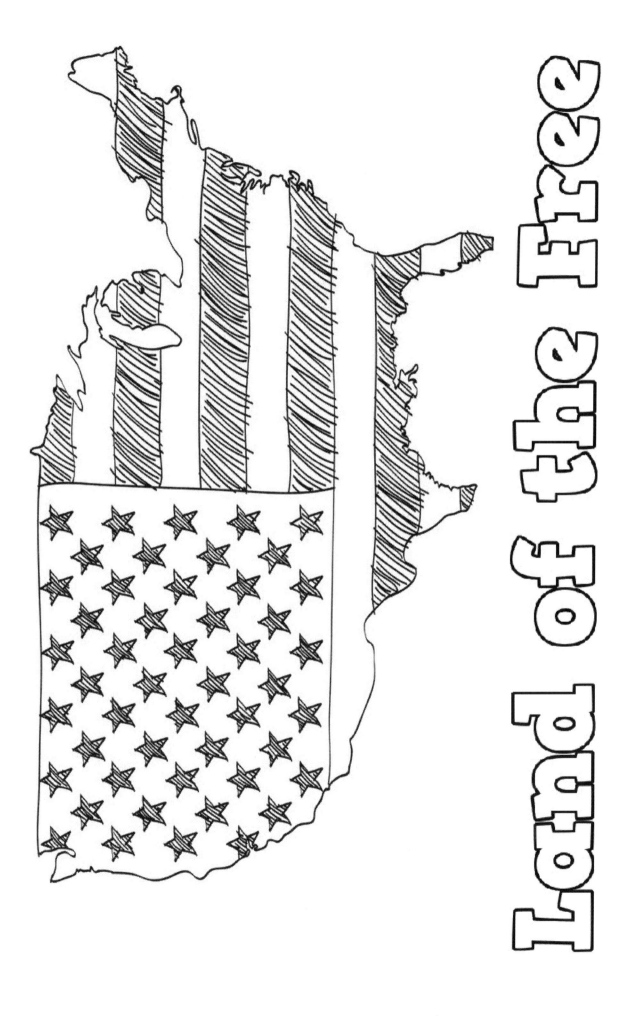

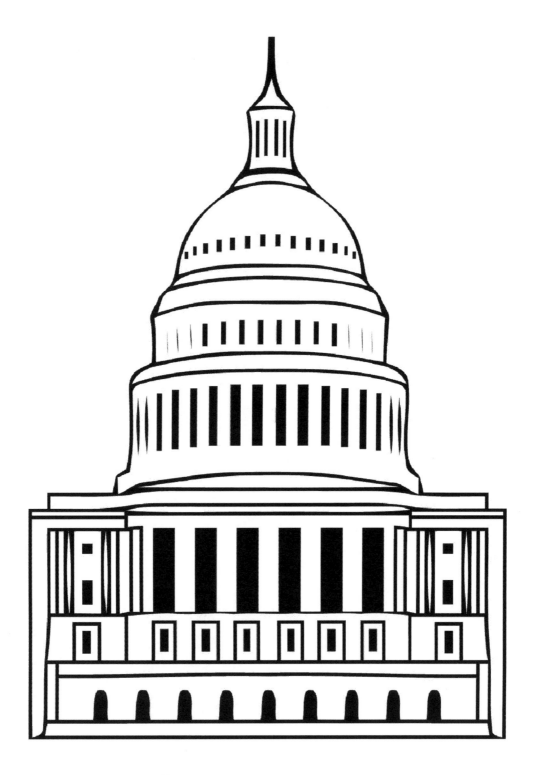

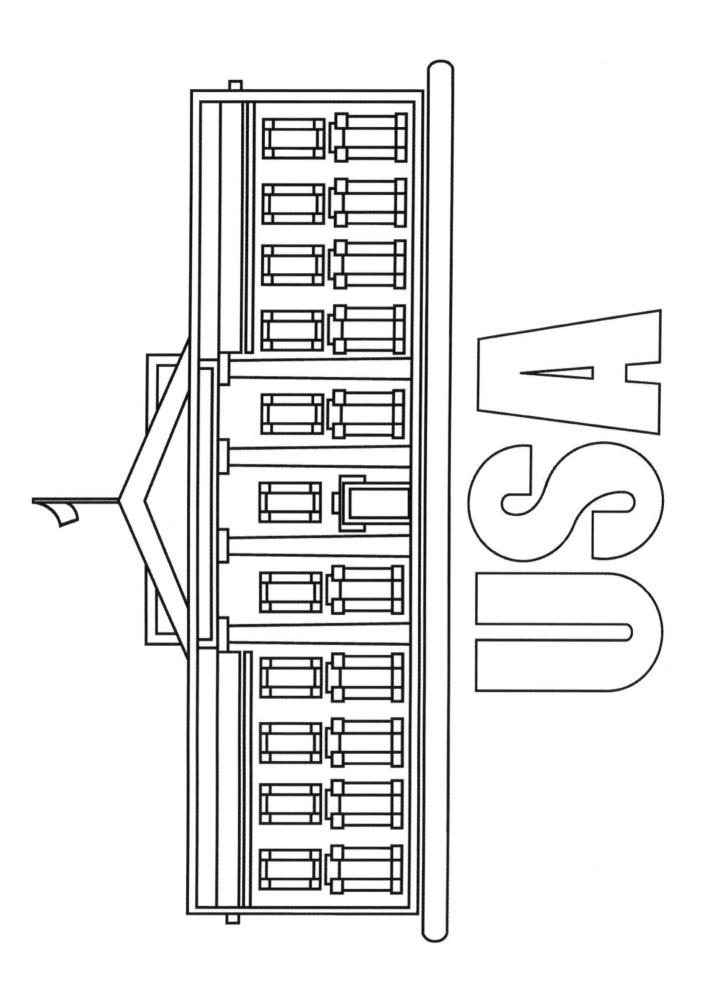

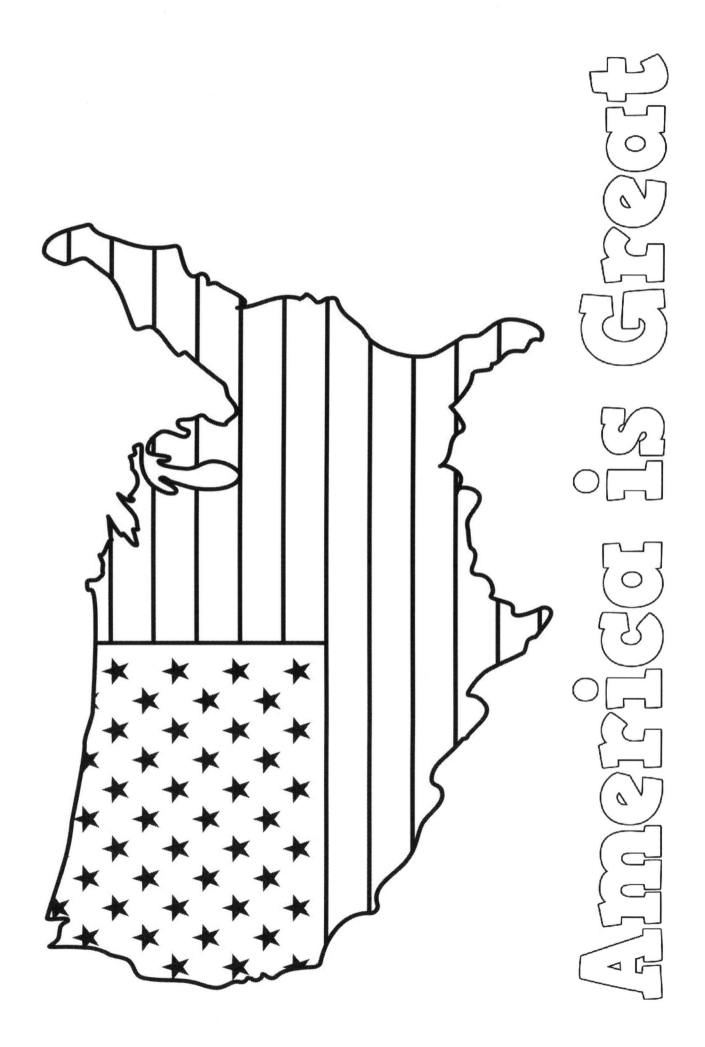

Bald Eagle

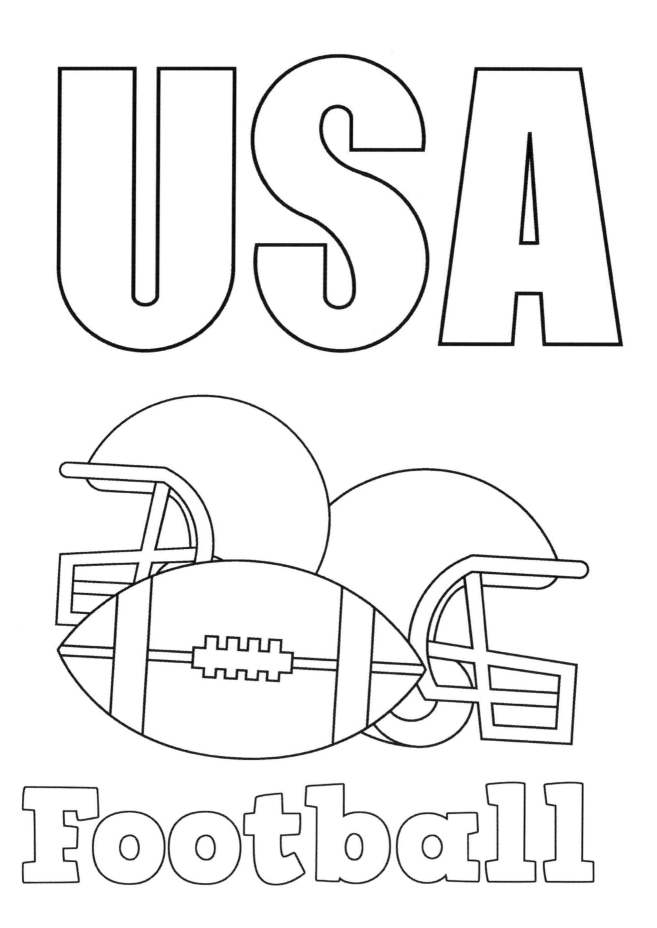

Uncle Sam

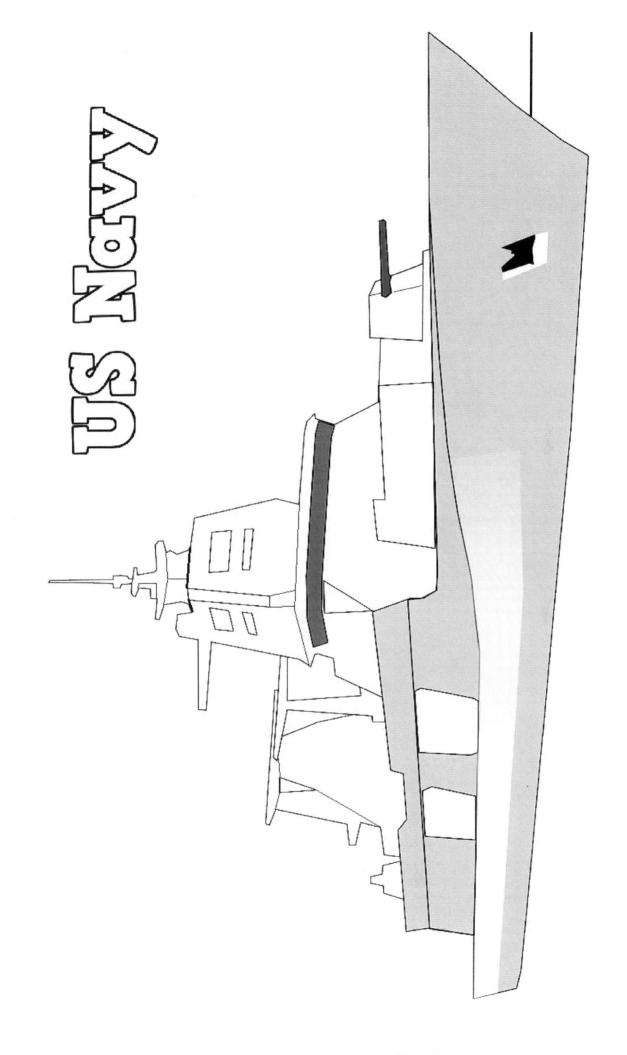

Happy Independence Day

Thank you for coloring with us
Happy Independence Day!!

(Please consider to rate & review this coloring book)

More from Rachel Mintz coloring books:

More from Rachel Mintz coloring books:

More from Rachel Mintz coloring books:

More from Rachel Mintz coloring books:

Look for Rachel Mintz Coloring Books

What is your favorite niche? What would you like to color?

Mandalas | Wildlife | Marine Life| **Portraits** | Dogs | Cats | **Flowers** | Skulls | Gothic | Architecture | Romantic | Texts & Sayings | Ethnic | Steampunk | **Fashion** | Horses | Unicorns | Witches | Horror | Grayscale | Sports | Christmas | Holidays | Kids | Cars | **Motorbikes** | Trucks | Urban | Fairies | **Jewish Holidays**: Passover, Hanukkah, Purim | Safari | Pets |Multicultural | Educational for Kids | Back to School | **Preschool & Toddlers** | Army & Military | Knights & Castles | Dragons | Princesses | Butterflies | Birds | Reptiles | Bible | **Stained Glass** | Abstract | Machines | **Robots** | Space & Science | **Zombies** | Monsters | And many more topics..

Search Amazon for Rachel Mintz coloring + your topic

Scan Code See Military **Digital Coloring Books** (PDF) For Kids & Adults: Tanks, Air Force, Marines, Special Forces and More.. **Instant download!** Color favorite pages again and again..

Made in the USA
Columbia, SC
17 April 2025

56758769R00059